visions

QuiltArt

Janet Rogers, Editor

QUILT SAN DIEGO

C&T Publishing

QUILT SAN DIEGO JURYING PHILOSOPHY

We define a work of art as a work that is in some way extraordinary. It is expressive and invites us to see ourselves and the world anew, or inspires us in a new way.

We want the best in quiltmaking today. It is certainly not our intention to shock the public. While it is important to represent the range of today's quiltmaking, it is equally important that each quilt possess a vitality of its own and be able to stand alone as well as work with the other quilts to provide an exhibition that somehow "gels" together.

We want the public to see a range of quilts, some that perhaps may initially "feel" familiar and also those that will make them stop and think, evoke an emotion, create an opinion. We want quilts that derive from the necessity to communicate—that speak from the soul of the quiltmaker.

We want quilts that flow with color, sparkle with excitement, those that make visual impacts, and those that are so subtle that one must look closely to see unusual use of fabric, high technical skills, and other marvelous effects used to create the design.

We want all those wonderful, incredible quilts that express the quiltmaker's creativity. We want an exhibit that compels the viewer to return for more than one look.

MISSION STATEMENT

Quilt San Diego is a not-for-profit international arts organization dedicated to the promotion and appreciation of the quilt as art.

Quilt San Diego will achieve its purpose by establishing a worldwide network of dedicated members, advisers, associates, and affiliates that will:
- organize and stage exhibitions of outstanding quilts in museum quality settings;
- present workshops, lectures, a contemporary quilt registry, and related activities to its members, the world arts community, and to the general public;
- promote presentations and discussions of the quilt as art in leading international art, quilting, and general circulation media; and
- encourage and promote quilting of the highest aesthetic and artistic quality.

ACKNOWLEDGMENTS

Quilt San Diego's most successful accomplishment has been the staging of the international biennial Visions exhibitions. Visions: QuiltArt would not have been possible without the countless hours of hard work provided by our dedicated volunteers. To everyone who contributed I extend my most sincere appreciation:

Will Chandler, Penny McMorris, and David Walker, Jurors;

Thayes Hower, Executive Director of Quilt San Diego;

Members of the Quilt San Diego Board of Directors: Lee Ann Decker, Merilyne Hickman, Gay Sinclair, Lucinda Eddy, Karen Bowden, Linda Gruber, Cecilia Stanford, Lois Hammond, Suzanne Appelman, and Jean Benelli;

Visions Committee Chairpersons: Merilyne Hickman, Lee Ann Decker, Linda Gruber, Harriet Love, Christen Brown, Phyllis Newton, and Stevii Graves;

The San Diego Historical Society and Lucinda Eddy;

Penny Nii;

Nihon Vogue Co., Ltd.;

C&T Publishing: Todd and Tony Hensley, Diane Pedersen, Lee Jonsson, Kathleen Lee, John Cram, and Diana Roberts;

Our generous corporate sponsors, members, and viewers who encourage us by coming back for more;

And finally, quiltmakers everywhere who happily submit *their* visions to Quilt San Diego so that we may fulfill *our* mission to you.

▲ **Janet Rogers**
President, Board of Directors
Quilt San Diego

AWARDS

Penny Nii Quilt Art Award

Contemporary quilting is a wonderful mixture of traditional techniques, designs, and materials. In the process of moving from the bed to the wall, the contemporary art quilt has become a unique art form. The Penny Nii Quilt Art Award has been established to encourage the artists working in this medium. The winning quilt was selected for its artistic merit by a judge chosen from the art world. It is hoped that the award will help artists focus on the art components of composition and color in addition to traditional craftsmanship and techniques.

Nihon Vogue Quilts Japan Award

Nihon Vogue is the sponsor of the Quilts Japan Award. The objective of the Quilts Japan Award is to express gratitude for the continued growth of the Japanese quilt, which is due greatly to American quilters, and to pay respect to the predecessors of quiltmaking. With this award, Nihon Vogue hopes to play a role in the development of quiltmaking by helping to link the ties between Japanese and American quiltmakers. The winner of the 1996 Quilts Japan Award is Ellen Oppenheimer.

©1996 Quilt San Diego

Editor: Janet Rogers
Developmental Editor: Lee Jonsson
Technical Editor: Diana Roberts
Copy Editor: Judith M. Moretz
Cover Design: Kathleen Lee
Book Design: John M. Cram
Photography: Carina Woolrich

Library of Congress Cataloging-in-Publication Data
Visions : quiltart / [Janet Rogers, project director].
   p. cm.
   "Quilt San Diego."
   ISBN 1-57120-021-5
   1. Quilts--United States--History--20th century--Exhibitions.
   I. Rogers, Janet. II. Quilt San Diego (Organization) III. Museum of San Diego History.
NK9112.V57 1996
746.46'074794985--dc20

96-28178
CIP

Published by C&T Publishing
P.O. Box 1456
Lafayette, CA 94549

Printed in Hong Kong
10 9 8 7 6 5 4 3 2 1

SAN DIEGO HISTORICAL SOCIETY PERSPECTIVE

The San Diego Historical Society proudly welcomes Quilt San Diego's fifth juried exhibition. Since 1990 the Society's Museum of San Diego History in Balboa Park has been the official host site for this extraordinary biennial exhibition of contemporary quilts. Beginning with Visions: A New Decade, San Diego Historical Society and Quilt San Diego developed a unique partnership that has resulted in unprecedented visitor attendance for the museum, and four successful collaborations between our two organizations. Today we are delighted to present Visions: QuiltArt, an exhibition of 80 exceptional works on fabric, representing the tremendous diversity, talent, and beauty which has elevated the medium of contemporary quiltmaking to fine art.

Founded in 1928, the San Diego Historical Society's mission has been to collect, preserve, exhibit, and interpret materials in order to promote the history of the San Diego region for the enlightenment and education of its residents and visitors. As a local and regional historical society, our mission is best fulfilled when we are able to communicate an understanding of the bonds that exist between our modern-day lives and the world of history. Through our publications, programs, and exhibitions the Society seeks to document our region's rich cultural history. In many ways Quilt San Diego's biennial exhibitions and catalogs have accomplished a similar mission by recording for future generations the contemporary art quilting movement of the late 20th century.

As San Diego's largest historical agency, we strive to present an accurate and meaningful interpretation of the diverse peoples who have influenced the development of our city and county through the material culture, photographic images, and written testimonies they have left over time. In a very similar fashion, the Visions exhibitions, through the medium of quilts, have brought to light a rich and eclectic tapestry of cultural influences which speak volumes about the contemporary society in which we live today. Through fabric, thread, and the creative process, modern-day quilters infuse their work with social commentary, using design, color, and an almost infinite variety of innovative techniques to boldly express their views on society, politics, and the environment. Today's quilters are also just as likely to use their medium to make profound personal statements, reflecting a wide range of emotions, from joy and humor, to disillusionment, grief, and loss. Others depict the psychological journeys taken toward greater self-knowledge. The results may delight, fascinate, puzzle, or even shock the viewer, but in every case, today's quiltmakers have demonstrated their link to the thousands of quilters whose patterns and techniques have evolved over the centuries into one of America's truly indigenous art forms.

Visions: QuiltArt is a remarkable exhibition. Its diversity, energy, and artistry attest to the skill, breadth, vitality, and inspiration that characterizes the best in quiltmaking today. The Visions quilts clearly illustrate new approaches being taken in this field and will challenge some viewers' more traditional concepts of the medium. These quilt artists have stretched the rules that once bound quiltmaking, and their work will engender some controversy and provoke thought about just what constitutes a quilt in the 1990s.

The thought, care, and talent that is so integral to this quilt exhibition is matched only by the tremendous effort Quilt San Diego has brought to the Visions project. Special thanks to the Board of Quilt San Diego and President Janet Rogers, and to Thayes Hower, Executive Director, for the enormous task of planning and executing every detail of this exhibition. Thanks also to the many tireless volunteers who have contributed their time and talents, making Visions a huge success.

▲ **Lucinda L. Eddy**
Associate Director
San Diego Historical Society

INTRODUCTION

Any international juried exhibition of contemporary art worth its salt presents a multitude of challenging questions. Is there a discernible cohesiveness among the works, or do many directions emerge? Does technique dominate meaning, or vice versa? Is there a maturity to the works, or do they seem experimental? Do we understand them? Do we like any of them?

Visions: QuiltArt presents some unique questions: How does this exhibition of contemporary quilts relate to exhibitions of fiber art, sculpture, or painting? Are we quiltmakers moving toward the mainstream themes of contemporary art, or are we carving out an aesthetic niche all our own? Which direction do the viewers identify with?

Dialogue today often centers around the issue of what is the appropriate direction for quiltmaking. As we quiltmakers aspire to have our quilts accepted as art, we will be trying to face all the issues that other media artists have to deal with. This means expressing through our quilts what we think about ourselves and how we view our world.

Artists have always acted as mirrors to the society in which they live. As artists comment on their society through their work, some do so with humor, some with irony. Some see and create with love, and some with anguish. Some speak of monumental conflicts and some express the simplest gestures of human compassion.

As we quilt artists attempt to move onto the main stage of the art world, we find the critical spotlight shining upon us, exposing our weaknesses as well as our strengths. Until now the quilt world has been protected from serious criticism; its work has been valued because all quiltmakers are valued. This "blanket" acceptance has provided a cocoon around quiltmakers, even art-quiltmakers.

Art quilters may be shocked when their work is challenged by critics who have their own motivations and agendas. But it is the critics' role to put artists in the uncomfortable position of defending themselves. Painful as this is, we are strengthened by such challenges. As part of this growth, we will learn to build up the self-protective calluses other artists get.

As quiltmakers move toward greater artistic expressiveness, quilt lovers will be challenged to understand and appreciate what these artists are doing. True art is always probing a little deeper into the unknown. For the viewers, the reward is learning to understand the artist's vision. Each quilt is an invitation to the viewer: a message encoded in cloth and thread, color and form, which reveals something interesting that was not known before. This message is not always the first thing that meets the eye. Often we must ponder a little. Squint. Walk away and come back. Secret messages are usually worth probing for.

Many of the fourteen million Americans who identify themselves as quiltmakers will continue to be content making the attractively sentimental quilts which please us all. However, it is the artists who are now more important to the vitality of quiltmaking than its tradition. It is the artists who will keep quiltmaking relevant as an exciting, creative form into the twenty-first century, rather than only a historical involvement with the past. New ideas first seen in exhibitions such as Visions: QuiltArt filter down through all levels of quiltmaking. A glance at the major quilt magazines quickly reveals how quilt artists' influences have changed quiltmaking in the past fifteen years.

We quiltmakers who submitted work for this exhibit, whether accepted this time or not, are brave souls who are taking on new challenges as we explore the universal questions of who we are and how we relate to each other.

I am encouraged to carry on, and I encourage my fellow artists to do so also. I am confident the risks we take will be worth it. I hope that fifty years from now our quilts will be studied, admired, and loved, as much as the paintings of our beloved Impressionists, which not so long ago were ridiculed, and now are treasured.

So, work hard, explorers!

Make quilts that set our hearts and minds aflame!

We can't wait to see them!

▲ **Jonathan Shannon**
Visions: QuiltArt Exhibitor

4

David Walker
Cincinnati, Ohio

David Walker has exhibited his work at dozens of venues, including Quilt National, Athens, Ohio; Quilt/Surface Design Symposium, Lancaster, Ohio; Art Quilt International '94, Mountain View, California; Quiltfest USA, Louisville, Kentucky; and Visions 1992: The Art of the Quilt, San Diego, California. He has presented lectures and workshops at numerous symposia and shows, most notably for several consecutive years at Quilt/Surface Design Symposium. He has been published in many quilting and other fiber-related as well as interior design magazines. David has received awards and recognition from several arts organizations, including Quilt National, the National Quilting Association, the Rockefeller Foundation, and "Best of 1988" by the Ohio Designer Craftsmen.

The art quilt. There has been so much written about the art quilt over the past three decades I find myself hard-pressed to arrive at something new and fresh to say. However, this is the plight of the quilt artist as well, isn't it? How to make the work fresh and invigorating, thought-provoking and inspirational, beautiful and important.

Sustaining the jurors' visual, emotional, and intellectual interest were important determining factors in the selection process. Was the work worthy of repetitive viewing? Did it speak with an interesting vocabulary? Was the work telling an old story with new words, or was it using old words to tell a new story? Was it provocative or thought provoking?

From this juror's perspective, I came to the jurying panel with the belief that anything that calls itself great art must be three things: beautiful, truthful, and transformative. Therefore, these three qualities guided my search for determining the final selection of quilts for the exhibition. To clarify, I believe great art exposes beauty in all its forms and manifestations, and since, in my mind, beauty and truth are synonymous, sometimes, the visually, emotionally, and intellectually ugly must, of its very nature, rise to the surface as truth, and hence as beauty. In addition, great art is transformative. It is a moving experience that removes us from the narrow venue of consciousness that surrounds us. It engenders an obvious assertion that the artist was transformed in some way during its making, and so the completed work also is able to transform the viewer in like fashion.

One further observation regarding the nature of great art is that it can often be illusive. It has already been a humbling experience for me to see actual work that did not make it into the exhibition and see in it the beauty, truth, and transformative energy that I had been searching for all along. I have learned that much wonderful and deserving work innocently slips through the cracks in the process. One should never give up hope regarding her or his artistic talent based on any one exhibit. The best advice is to keep working, keep trying, and keep believing in yourself above all else.

What about the use of new techniques and methods, fabric manipulations, experimentation with the medium, and other similar considerations? The expert use of any of these does not make a person an artist, nor does it make a particular quilt a work of art. When a particular technique, no matter how innovative and mind-boggling, attempts to take center stage, it tends to subtract rather than add to the creative outcome. Whatever methods and materials are used in the making of any art quilt, each must be used with a sensitivity to its subject matter and add to the integrity of the entire piece. In all cases the work must be well-constructed, whether it is executed by hand or by machine.

The final selection of quilts for Visions: QuiltArt represents a cross-section of what is happening in the work of art quilts today. I believe the exhibition has something for everyone. There are quilts you will surely identify as great examples of quilt art, and I am sure there will be a few quilts that will cause you to question the jurors' sanity! All in all, the exhibit is represented by a well-balanced combination of established quilt artists as well as many newcomers to the scene. It is my hope that everyone who views Visions: QuiltArt will in some way find beauty and honesty and somehow be transformed by the experience.

I would like to take this opportunity to thank Quilt San Diego for inviting me to participate as one of the jurors for Visions: QuiltArt. I thoroughly enjoyed working with Penny McMorris and Will Chandler. I applaud both of them for their cooperative spirit and willingness to share their wealth of experience. From an artist's perspective, I have grown greatly from the experience and now have a greater understanding of just how difficult and gut-wrenching a juror's job can be. I also wish to thank all the quilt artists who entered work into the exhibition and to especially congratulate those who succeeded through the final round. I consider it a privilege to have viewed the work of so many dedicated quilt artists.

Penny McMorris
Bowling Green, Ohio

Penny McMorris is currently a consultant to Owens-Corning Fiberglas Corporation for their 1,000 piece art collection. She is also a consultant to a major private collector of contemporary quilts. She is a partner in The Electric Quilt Company, a software firm producing computer software for quilt design.

She has advised and guest-curated several contemporary quilt gallery exhibits including Nancy Crow: Improvisational Quilts. Penny, who has an M.A. in Art History, has produced and hosted three PBS series on quilts, and written two books, *Crazy Quilts*, and *The Art Quilt*.

Jurying any exhibition is an honor. Ever since I first became interested in quilts, nearly twenty-five years ago, my overwhelming desire has been to see the best new original quilt designs being made. So, having a chance to jury a show with the stature of Visions: QuiltArt is at once an intense pleasure and an incredible opportunity. I'd like to thank Quilt San Diego Executive Director Thayes Hower, and President Janet Rogers, and the whole exhibition committee for letting me be part of this year's jury, and Will and David for showing me new insights and for being such fun.

Jurying is also a great responsibility. I am always aware of the hopes accompanying the submitted slides. David, Will, and I knew our decisions would disappoint nine out of ten entrants. That was never far from our minds as we made our decisions. And since so many quilts are rejected and so few are accepted, it's only natural to wonder just what it is a jury is looking for.

To understand the difference between work that gets accepted and that which is rejected, you must first realize what jurors are looking at. They're not reading your artist's statement. They don't know your name, or see your résumé listing what classes you've taken, what shows you've been in, or even what prizes you've won. They know only what they see. And what they see is a few slides.

Jurors sit in a dark room, staring at the wall, and suddenly it's your turn—you're on. For fifteen seconds or so, two reproductions of your quilt flash on the screen. The quality of your slides is critical. I can remember only a few instances where quilts with poor slides made the final cut. In general, the more professional the slides, the more professional the artist.

Once your slides are on, a juror compares your work to everything else submitted. That's your competition. The worst thing you could do is base your quilt design on your impression of what the judges picked the previous year. To make your own work stand out, it is vitally important to develop a style of your own. That way, when others are aping the latest trends,

colors, and techniques, your work will have an impact because it's not the fortieth example they've seen. This year a great many entries followed three current trends: fractured landscapes in blues and greens; box-within-box block-style compositions in warm colors; and painterly collages. There were few traditional quilts, even though Visions exhibitions intend to represent the wide range of quiltmaking today, including innovative approaches to traditional designs (e.g., Carol Gersen's *Zig-Zag Log Cabin*).

How do you develop your own style? Perhaps you need to put on blinders. Whereas the quilt world was once so small, now it's nearly impossible to keep from being bombarded by influences. Today there are more quilting magazines, exhibitions, classes, books, and even Internet chat groups than one person could ever take in. My advice to anyone truly wanting to develop as an artist may sound radical, but I really believe it: Shut out the quilting world for awhile. The most important thing you may be able to do for your work in the next several years is ignore every quilt-related activity going on around you and concentrate solely on doing your own work and developing your own voice.

Once you master techniques, stop taking classes. Focus completely on doing your own work and learning from it. You must become your own teacher and critic. Listen to the artist Jim Dine, who at a peak in his career withdrew to the studio to concentrate on improving his ability to draw. "I have great confidence in my drawing …I didn't always have it…I specifically sat down to train myself." He spent six years drawing, erasing, drawing, day after day. "I've learned how to sense what is needed to correct, and to love correcting," he says.

Above all, believe in yourself. Remember, many artists you may admire have been working for fifteen to twenty years to accomplish what they have. Yes, they have talent. They also have a willingness to devote themselves completely to hard work, introspection, and improvement. They believed they were artists; then they worked hard to become so. So can you. Good luck.

Will Chandler

San Diego, California

Will Chandler is proprietor of Chandler Art Consulting Services in San Diego, California. His consultancy includes personal property appraisal, art preservation, and architectural history research. A 1973 graduate of the University of California at Berkeley's College of Environmental Design (B.A. Design; Textiles and Design History), he was Associate Curator of Decorative Arts at the San Diego Museum of Art from 1976 to 1988. While at SDMA, he provided technical analysis and conservation for the Binney Quilt Collection, and was curator of that collection's touring exhibition, "Homage to Amanda," for the Smithsonian Institution's Traveling Exhibition Service. The exhibition was seen by more than 600,000 people in fourteen museums across the United States.

When I was invited to participate on the jury for Quilt San Diego's Visions: QuiltArt exhibition, I was at once delighted and apprehensive. The success of this exhibition and its international popularity with quilt artists promised a challenging and probably grueling selection process. However, the experience and professionalism of the members of Quilt San Diego were justly reassuring. The exhibition committee's organizational skills and detailed preparations were evident at every stage of the project.

We jurors arrived to find we would be viewing dual slides for some 850 entries. What might have been an exhausting and confusing experience was instead all that one might hope for. Meticulous notes on each entry, lightning resorting of the slide trays, and a ready supply of refreshments kept us alert, relaxed, and focused on the works themselves.

I am equally grateful to my fellow jurors Penny McMorris and David Walker. Their multi-faceted experience with contemporary quilting and of art history, and their readiness to discuss and debate the images before us happily and candidly, allow me to believe that we did all that was possible to choose the finest examples submitted to us. While our tastes differed widely, we shared the understanding that we were working in the service of all of the entrants. Not surprisingly, we found there were many pieces we yearned to see "in the cloth," and a few pieces we deeply admired and, in the end, could not include.

My own background includes a degree in textile design and design history and twelve years as the decorative arts director of a moderately large museum. My primary involvement with quilts has been the preservation, technical evaluation, and exhibition of historical examples dating from around 1745 through the beginning of the twentieth century.

With this in mind, let me say that the field of entries to Visions: QuiltArt demonstrated the astonishing amount of good work being done internationally in the various quilt media. Each juror must bring his or her own standards and prejudices to the table. I have mine, and like my co-jurors, I strive not to take all of my own ideas too seriously. I tend to gripe that many fiber artists over the past twenty years have wanted their textile pieces to look as much like corporate gallery paintings as possible. When I go on to think that this is a fiber arts problem, I hope I am quick to remember the problem is more mine than it is the art world's.

If I must define the kind of pieces in any art medium I am not eager to see in an exhibition, I use the phrase "stuff that looks like art." By this I mean in part that there are contemporary artists who seem much too concerned with producing works that fit the public's (and their own) mass-media-influenced notions of what art looks like. They have their points and their rights, but I want to see works that both express and transcend knowledge of techniques, and which take us all somewhere wonderful that no other piece has and that no other piece can.

However they might express it, I believe that as jurors we were united in this concern. When the selection was completed, we could stand together delighted with the variety and quality of what had been presented to us, and which we present to you.

8

Ellen Oppenheimer
Oakland, California

Labyrinth #5
75″ x 75″

Silk-screened and dyed cotton fabrics

Machine-sewn, hand-quilted

Labyrinth #5 is part of a series. I was interested in working with more palatable colors than those I had used in previous work. In this series I work with a continuous line. The closed loop line represents an aesthetic decision and an emotional allegory. The geometric and linear possibilities in this format seem boundless and intriguing.

Ellen Oppenheimer has won the 1996 Nihon Vogue Quilts Japan Award for *Labyrinth #5*.

I've recently begun dyeing my own fabrics, and it seemed appropriate to use the first of these to depict the splendor of zinnias.

Constance Norton
Fairfax, Virginia

Zinnias for Iris
71.5″ x 71.5″

Cotton fabrics, hand-dyed by the artist, cotton batting

Machine-pieced and machine-quilted

Cynthia Corbin
Woodinville, Washington

Shape of Spirit
52″ x 76″

Cotton fabrics, cotton, metallic, and cotton-polyester thread

Machine-pieced, machine-quilted

To make visible that which we cannot see, to give form to the pulse and vibration of energy as it feels to me, was the challenge I undertook with *Shape of Spirit*. I strove for the quality I think of as "buzz." This piece encompasses a lot of what I think about the nature of "spirit" and its existence in everything we are and do. It surrounds us.

I began *Shape of Spirit* with a particular focus on shape—the shape of the elements used to build this quilt were to be interesting and thoughtful. I worked directly on the wall when designing this piece, not worrying about how it was going to go together, simply placing the shapes where I wanted them. During the process of machine-piecing I did the fine-tuning to make it all fit together.

Eternal Horizons is a memorial quilt for the seven children who perished in the bus and train accident which happened less than a mile from my home. Our communities of Cary and Fox River Grove have been grieving over the loss; this quilt is a way of working toward healing for me, and hopefully represents hope for the family members and friends of the young people involved. Although I knew none of the victims, in small towns like ours everyone one feels compassion for the families that suffer such losses.

The seven side panels represent the seven teens and the center panel is their eternal horizon. I wanted it to be hopeful and bright, reminding all that our time here is short and eternity awaits.

Melody Johnson
Cary, Illinois

Eternal Horizons
99″ x 80.5″

Cotton fabrics hand-dyed by the artist, fusible web, rayon machine embroidery threads

Pieced, bonded, machine-quilted

Linda Colsh

Salinas, California

In the Hot Seat

56" x 63"

Domestic and Thai cotton fabrics, cotton, rayon, and metallic threads

Machine-pieced, machine-quilted

In the Hot Seat is where my friend Lucretia and I found ourselves during a trip to northern Thailand. Unwittingly, we went at the start of the opium shipping season—a dangerous time. Rifle-toting Thai rangers manned "tourist" security outposts in the mountains where we visited remote hill-tribe villages. At night, barking dogs and gunfire around our hotel made sleep impossible. We should have gone on this trip during a safer time, but getting out unscathed made the trip an adventure.

But why chairs? At the time, I was living in Korea, a floor-sitting culture. When something is missing it becomes significant by its very absence. The chair is stable, a place to rest. But in the musical game, the chair is not guaranteed. As we travel around the chairs, "chair anxiety" and excitement increase: Will there be a chair for me or not?

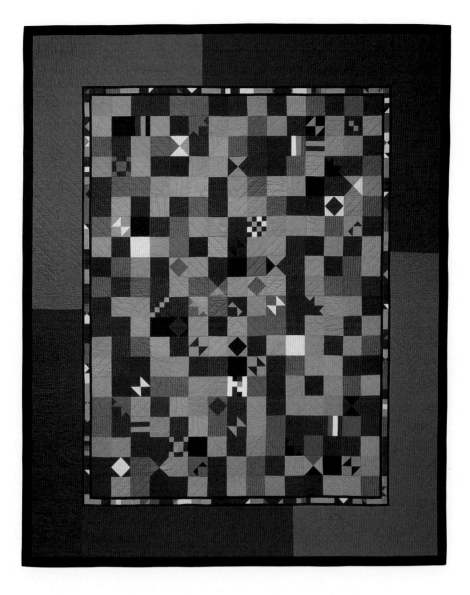

It is quite motivating to an aspiring artist to have a nationally-respected artist whose work you admire encourage you and admire your work. For me, that person is Robert Stark, the owner of The Art Exchange, a non-profit facility dedicated to fostering the growth of the arts in the rural area. There I was re-introduced to the color theory of Josef Albers and explored the work of traditional and contemporary artists. In addition to being very generous with his help, Bob spurred me to push my boundaries in my quilting.

Color Exploration is part of a series using four-inch solid color fabrics. I enjoy deep, saturated colors and the interaction in this piece between the solid and pieced blocks. The shapes and colors provide visual stimulation. The quilting toys with tradition. Like the goldfish that grows to the boundaries of its bowl, I think of the quilting here as playfully bouncing against the confines of the piecing.

Veronica Haberthuer
Honesdale, Pennsylvania

Color Exploration
88″ x 108″

All cotton fabrics, Warm and Natural™ cotton batting

Machine-pieced, hand-quilted

13

14

Melissa Holzinger
Arlington, Washington

Patch of Blue Ground
36″ x 45″

Canvas, acrylic paint, pastels, charcoal, waxed linen

Hand-painted, machine-appliquéd, machine-quilted

Patch of Blue Ground is part of a series of works I call Internal Landscapes.

Motion and energy were the driving forces in creating this piece. The various shapes and forms dancing and playing on the surface draw the eye across the quilt and the heat generated by the dramatic, hot background colors draw the viewer into it. Don't forget to wear your sunscreen!

Jan Rickman
Cary, Illinois

SPF 25
39″ x 58.5″

Commercial and hand-dyed cotton fabrics

Fuse-appliquéd, free-motion-embroidered, machine-pieced and quilted

Susan Webb Lee
Weddington, North Carolina

Missy's New Clothes
37″ x 45″

Cotton fabrics, hand-painted and hand-dyed fabrics
by various artists

Machine-pieced, machine-appliquéd, hand-
embroidered, machine-quilted

I began this quilt at Arrowmont School during its 50th anniversary celebration. Forty-four other former faculty members took part in this magical week of collaborating, sharing, and reaffirming their creative energies. We forged into each others' studios, immersing ourselves in familiar and unfamiliar media. Many delightful fabrics were painted for me by the other artists, some of which are included in this quilt.

In an effort to continue this spirit of intense creative passion, I have dedicated this quilt to my friend, Sylvain Klaus, whose immense courage, strength, and "zest for life" have been an immeasurable source of inspiration for me and countless others. Sylvain faced the daily tragedy of living with AIDS, but he resolutely continued his productive and well-respected career as an artist. His story is one of hope and dedication, and is a tribute to self-determination.

Sylvain died on May 7, 1996.

My constant companion during the cold, gray days of December in Illinois is an old blue velvet chair that sits across from me as I read. It is like an elderly member of the family, treasured and admired for its antique poise. One day I pictured my blue chair reading along with me. Its selection was a text on the Blue Book value of blue chairs. Since then, I have made the blue chair appear in several poses, *Nude Blue Chair Reclining, Blue Beach Chair,* and *Green Tea and Blue Chair.* The Blue Chair series is like most of my quilts, whimsical in nature, with festive colors, humorous stories, fanciful perspective.

Laura Wasilowski
Elgin, Illinois

Blue Book on Blue Chairs
46″ x 57″

Hand–dyed cotton fabrics, hand-dyed perle cotton thread, textile ink

Machine-appliquéd, machine-quilted, couched rayon ribbon, ink-stamped

Marcia Anop-Romashko
Mequon, Wisconsin

Frangiapani Marauder
80″ x 102″

Cotton fabrics, metallic and rayon thread, oil pastels

Painted, pieced, appliquéd, embroidered, machine-quilted

Frangiapani Marauder is a synthesis of several elements: my emotional response to the color and pattern in the fabric and my study of myths through the writings of Joseph Campbell. This piece recounts a story about a hefty, six-inch, lime-green and black striped caterpillar I saw crawling along the ground in the British Virgin Islands.

A native Virgin Islander told me that this frightening yet beautiful creature is called the "frangiapani marauder" because it eats all the leaves and flowers of the frangiapani tree, which forces the plant into its required dormancy.

My quilt celebrates the fearsome yet miraculous realization that life comes from death.

For many years our family enjoyed owning a family cottage and property on Lake Huron in southern Ontario, Canada, 1300 miles east of our home in Winnipeg. Summer was eagerly anticipated each year as we looked forward to vacation days of sun on the water and dazzling sunsets at night. The painted sunset segment of this quilt is the sunset of the last night we walked the beach the year the cottage was sold.

Thanks for the Memories—Kintail, on which I have used personal slides, photo-transfer, and hand-painting techniques, pays tribute to many years of visual, sensual, and never-to-be-forgotten memories.

Much of my ongoing work in 1995 has been assisted by a Manitoba Arts Council grant, for which I express much appreciation.

Marilyn Stewart Stothers
Winnipeg, Manitoba, Canada

Thanks for the Memories–Kintail
65.5″ x 38.5″

Cotton fabrics and cotton threads

Photo-transferred, hand-painted with acrylic paint and pastels, machine-pieced, machine-quilted, hand-finished

19

Vicki L. Johnson
Soquel, California

On the Way Home
54″ x 46″

Cotton fabrics, fabric paint, various threads, including silk

Painted, soft-edge appliquéd, hand-appliquéd, machine-quilted

As I drive home from Monterey I often see this barn in the sunset. The barn in the quilt is soft-edge appliquéd and the sunset, meadow, and trees are painted with fabric paints. I "printed" the meadow in many colors with plastic wrap. The frame of two-inch squares are hand-appliquéd so they look as though they have been inserted into the scene. They were inspired by a handkerchief which I inherited from my mother that has quarter-inch squares in one of its borders. The machine quilting brings out the colors and shapes of the painting with colored thread.

Because I am a natural science illustrator, my work reflects my interest in biology and nature. This piece is a depiction of the flora and fauna of the Sonoran Desert. I was inspired to make *The Sonoran Desert* after my trip to the Arizona-Sonoran Desert Museum.

Jane Herbst
Lake Oswego, Oregon

The Sonoran Desert
65.5″ x 54″

Hand-dyed cotton fabrics, cotton batting, cotton thread

Machine-embroidered and machine-appliquéd

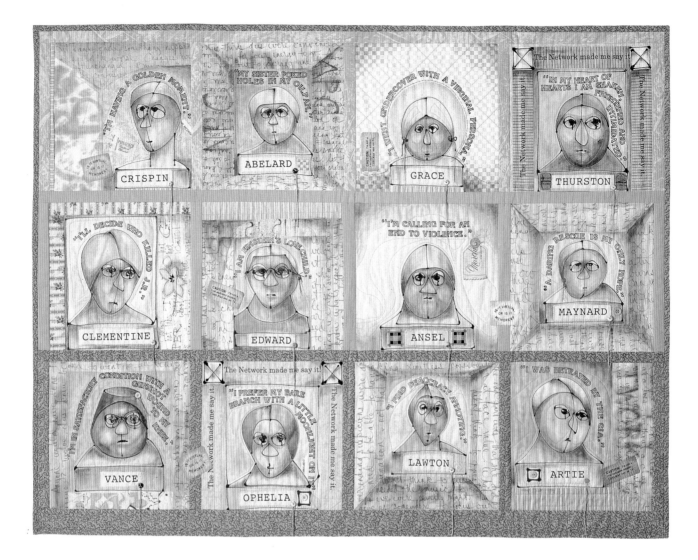

Gerry Chase
Seattle, Washington

Sampler IV: Play TV
59″ x 46″

Cotton and linen fabrics, India ink, acrylic paint

Pieced, appliquéd, drawn, painted, computer-processed

In *Play TV* the grid is a visual reference to the game show "What's My Line?" It sets the stage, so to speak, for developing my underlying idea that television has profoundly affected the way we think. No longer awkward or shy, we respond to the presence of a TV camera with remarkable aplomb—as if, mentally, we have rehearsed for the occasion. Let an accident befall us, and we can tell about it with the same dispassionate and precise attention to detail as would the evening news anchor. We are ordinary people, yet we can display our inner selves on the public stage as though it were, well, as easy as playing a part in a soap opera.

The text was the result of a two-week period of talk-show viewing.

Drop Cloth is part of a series of works which employs symbolic narrative to suggest the nature of inner realities. As in a dream, metaphors are to be decoded through the viewer's contextual reading of archetypal images.

Risë Nagin
Pittsburgh, Pennsylvania

Drop Cloth
78″ x 84″

Cotton and polyester fabrics, acrylic paint, heat-bond textile glue, colored pencils, thread

Stained and dyed fabrics, pieced, appliquéd, pierced, glued, hand-sewn

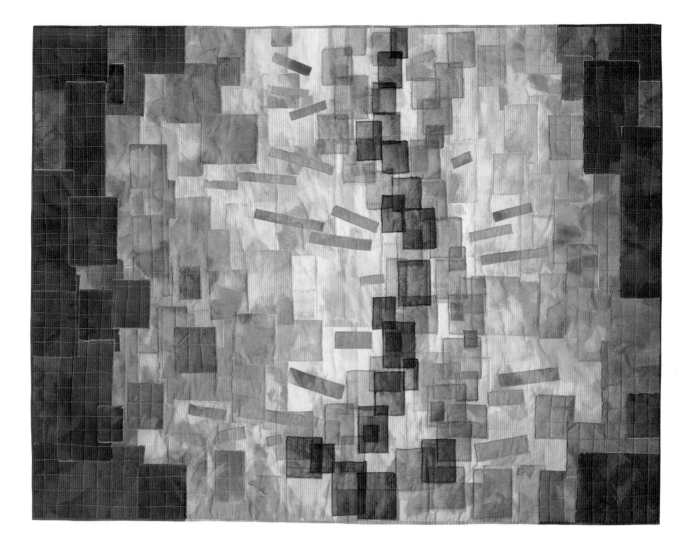

Erika Carter
Bellevue, Washington

Epiphany
61″ x 46″

Hand-painted silk organza and cotton fabrics,
painted by the artist

Torn fabric, directly machine-appliquéd

Epiphany continues my Support series that incorporates a line of silk organza squares to suggest a backbone. While referencing the human body, the backbone is a metaphor for support and strength. In *Epiphany* this backbone appears to vibrate with the dance of discovery, the moment of enlightenment.

I first saw the Royal Palms grove at my granddaughter's schoolyard in Maui, Hawaii. The palm's beautiful form contrasted sharply against the blue sky. The intricacy of pattern and color were my inspiration. I have used nature as the basis for many of my artworks.

Nature is the inspiration. The design is original.

Virginia Gaz
Cincinnati, Ohio

Royal Palms of Paia
32″ x 47.5″

Cotton and cotton-blend fabrics, rayon and metallic threads, fabric paints

Appliquéd and hand-painted

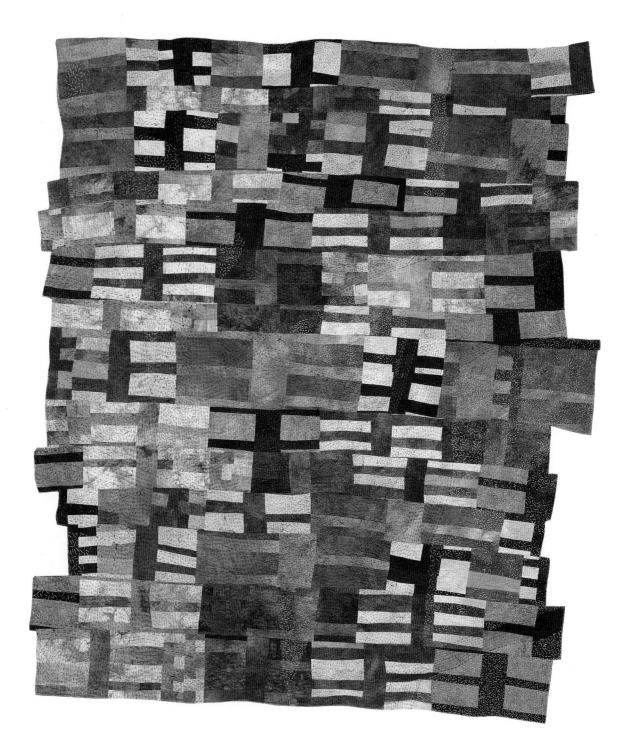

Pat Sims
Anchorage, Alaska

Forest and the Trees
72″ x 86.5″

Cotton fabrics, hand-dyed by the artist

Pieced and quilted

My work is deeply influenced by the many years I have lived in Alaska. I strive to express the immediacy and clarity of connection between humankind and nature. I design to capture the essence of a feeling or of a moment. Raw edges, frayed edges, and unclipped threads contribute to the spontaneity I find so important to reflect the power and simplicity of nature's beauty.

Forest and the Trees is one of an ongoing series of pieced and appliquéd works reflecting the power and mystery of a virgin forest. Using my own hand-dyed fabric I endeavor to immerse the viewer in a forest.

I love all the seasons, their colors and their moods. But spring is the season that influenced this piece. Spring is forever optimistic. This quilt is about hope, growth, renewal, and creative energy.

The "tree of life" is a universal symbol, and needleworkers from many cultures have interpreted it. Thus, this quilt pays its respects to generations of artists and craftspeople who have felt the need to express their ideas with fiber.

Jane A. Sassaman
Chicago, Illinois

Tree of Life–Spring
70″ x 80″

Cotton and cotton-blend fabrics

Appliquéd on whole-cloth background

Ann M. Adams
San Antonio, Texas

Natural Soul
39.5″ x 39″

Cotton velveteen fabrics, discharge dye, paint, metallic thread, cotton batting, cotton backing, silk crêpe de Chine

Block-printed, discharge-dyed, silk-screened, clamped and dyed, dyed with direct application of dye, machine-quilted

Natural Soul is about being in San Antonio in the heat of summer when you can feel the pulse of things living and growing. The air is heavy and resonates with the din of thousands of cicadas. I cut a series of wood blocks depicting images of commonplace things I encounter in my backyard. I have elevated these things to "art" to pay tribute to them. It is in my small, contemplative garden that I connect with the soul of nature and feel whole again.

Natural Soul is owned by the San Antonio Blood and Tissue Center.

The Fish in the Stream series was strongly influenced by my father's love of fishing. He fished as a meditation exercise rather than as a sport. I never cared to fish, but I came to understand his joy in their watery worlds and wild movements. The image of fish in water has become a metaphor for moving through life. This series represents myself and people I've known at different times of my life.

Twilight Pond heralded the meeting of an old friend. Sometimes meetings between old friends are not always what one hopes for. Sometimes the life changes are too great, or our memories re-wire so much of a person that real contact shatters past illusions. Time changes us, but our memories change the most easily, fitting comfortably into current beliefs, forgetting the reality of the past.

Ellen Anne Eddy
Chicago, Illinois

Twilight Pond
57″ x 54″

Hand-dyed cotton fabrics, iridescent and regular organza, tulle, rayon, metallic, iridescent, and nylon thread, novelty yarn, wool batting

Hand-dyed, machine-pieced, machine-quilted and embroidered, embroidered appliqué, couched thread

Me We Hu Tzing
Cannon Beach, Oregon

It's All Pink on the Inside
56.5″ x 51″

Hand-dyed cottons, silks, commercial fabrics, beads, paint

Painted, dyed, machine-pieced, machine- and hand-quilted, embroidered

It's All Pink on the Inside is one of a series of pieces that explore that timeless question: "What are little girls really made of?"

The Guns Are Us series reflects my concern about the conditions of violence that permit gunshot wounds to be one of the top killers of children. Increasing poverty, the prevalence of drugs, the greed of the gun dealers, the disparity of education, and the absence of real programs to begin to cure this society-eating virus of violence all point toward a dark and foreboding entry to the new millennium. The way we treat the most vulnerable members of our society tells the story for the society as a whole.

Guns Are Us: Funerary Piece Three is in memory of the girls and young women who have been innocent victims of violence in Chicago in the last year. From this series came the Dream Quilt Project where each girl made her own quilt illustrating her hopes for the future.

Kathy Weaver
Highland Park, Illinois

Guns Are Us: Funerary Piece Three
54″ x 47″

Cotton and satin fabrics, toy embellishments

Painted, color-xerographed, appliquéd, silk-screened, machine-pieced and quilted

Sharon Heidingsfelder
Little Rock, Arkansas

Paradise by Design
71.5″ x 89.5″

Cotton fabrics, some dyed by Elouise Gomez, Pine
Bluff, Arkansas, or silk-screened by the artist

Silk-screened, traditionally-pieced

I find it difficult to put my thoughts about my quilts
into words. I am, however, convinced of the merit of
contemporary art quilts. I enjoy the varied works of
other contemporary quilt artists who are creating quilts
that represent our times. Without this commitment to
new patterns and designs, I feel there would be no 20th-
century quilts, only reproductions of old quilts.

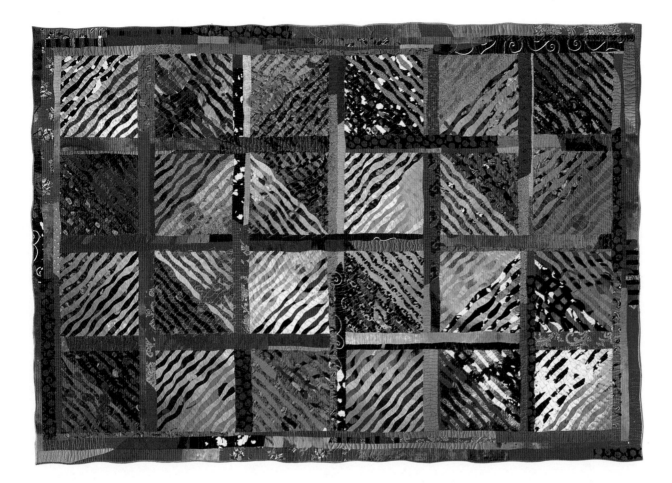

As a mother of two small children, I have been amazed and amused by how much of my brain is occupied with keeping a watchful eye on them.

When not worrying about my children, I love discovering similarities in folk patterns that cross cultural boundaries. I see these common elements as a sort of universal visual language.

The first quilt in this series was based on a traditional American quilt pattern, a Roman Stripe variation. The diamond shapes reminded me of the Mexican Eye of God. When I was a teenager, my mother and I made many of these yarn ornaments to decorate a Christmas tree. A few years ago I bought a beautiful book entitled *African Canvas* and became fascinated by the similar patterns painted by the Igbo women of Nigeria on the walls of their homes. These concentric diamonds are derived from a scarification pattern called Ogalu. Later quilts in this series, including this one, incorporate all of these ideas.

Sue Benner
Dallas, Texas

Watchful Eye IV: Ogalu
63″ x 43″

Commercial silks and dyes

Dyed, fused, machine-quilted

Elizabeth Barton
Athens, Georgia

Windows XVII: Oculus
71.5″ x 48″

Cotton fabrics, many dyed by the artist

Hand-dyed, machine-pieced, machine- and hand-appliquéd, machine-quilted, hand-quilted

"Oculus," a dome-top circular window, is Latin for "eye"—seeing light, seeking light, transmitting light.

I've been working on a series (including over twenty works, with more ideas in my head) exploring the qualities of light, space, and color using windows as a theme. The effects of light, and patterns of light and shade fascinate me. In this quilt I particularly wanted to convey a sense of space. I'm working on a similar idea on a larger scale for the Atlanta airport.

Wherever I go, I always seek the light. I want to see and know as much as I can!

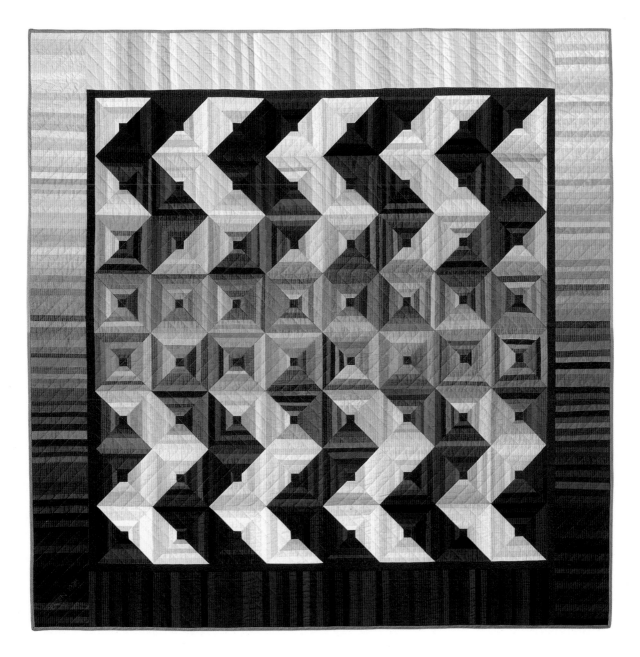

Zig-Zag Log Cabin relates to another of my quilts, *Rivers In the Sky*, which used only two colors, blue and red. Here I have made use of many of the fabrics I dyed over the past seven years to create a similar quilt in full color. *Zig-Zag Log Cabin* relates to the frequent thunderstorms that occur in western Maryland and the way that they connect earth and sky. This idea was brought to my mind when I read the first sentence of Zora Neale Hurston's *Jonah's Gourd Vine*: "God was grumbling his thunder and playing the zig-zag lightning through his fingers."

This piece is part of the collection of John M. Walsh III.

Carol Hemphill Gersen
Boonsboro, Maryland

Zig-Zag Log Cabin
72″ x 72″

Hand-dyed cotton fabrics

Machine-pieced, hand-quilted, signed and dated in quilting on the top

Emilie M. Belak
Danville, Washington

In Praise of Poppies
45.5″ x 57″

Cotton fabric, cotton, polyester, and metallic thread

Each petal was painted separately with fiber-reactive dyes and then embroidered with many red threads. The front petals are three-dimensional and gravity alone makes them open forward. Richly machine-embroidered leaves, flower buds, and seed pods complete this machine-quilted piece. The background fabric was painted by Caryl Bryer-Fallert.

My love of color, flowers, and Georgia O'Keefe's paintings inspired the creation of *In Praise of Poppies*. When the early spring flowers, crocuses, primroses, daffodils, and tulips start fading, much bolder irises, lupines, and Oriental poppies burst forth with the colors of summer. The gentle breezes and warm sun rays caress the body and soul and awaken the soil after the cold winter months. I appreciate and rejoice in every summer day, enjoying the colors of the flowers, buzz of bees, and songs of birds. The summer seems to pass all too quickly!

I was hooked on the idea of using Georges Seurat's *Sunday in the Park* painting solely with the Pointillist Palette™ after a suggestion from Debra Lunn that I do a quilt in my style using Lunn Studios' new line of fabric.

Uncomfortable with the idea of simply copying, I chose to advance some of the figures to a more modern time—the 20th century. The clothing is different but not dramatically so, as I wanted to keep the change subtle! By combining the centuries I was able to keep the grass and add some futuristic details, such as the floating video screen and keyboard, the vintage boombox, a futuristic Coke® can, and the modern dog collars. I did change body positions on some of the people so they appear to be aware of and/or shocked by the time travelers—both past and future.

Kathy Davie
Denver, Colorado

Georges Seurat Meets the Next Generation
46″ x 29.5″

Pointillist Palette™ cotton fabrics, velvet, DMC® embroidery floss, dyes, paint

Dyed, painted, hand-appliquéd, machine-pieced, hand-embroidered, machine-quilted

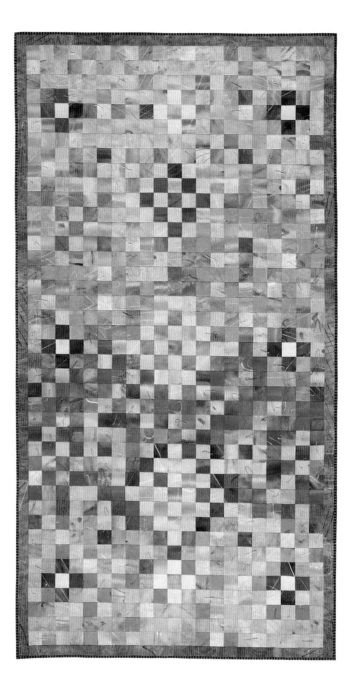

Mary Allen Chaisson
South Harpswell, Maine

Read the Earth
44″ x 83″

Cottons and blends, commercially painted fabrics, acrylic fabric paint and dye, cotton batting, and embroidery thread

Acrylic-washed, fabric paint-dyed, machine-pieced and hand-tied

The colors and natural beauty of the southwest inspired this piece, which is a tribute to the land and all that it provides for us. The design is my interpretation of a Navajo rug. Nine-patch squares contribute to the overall design. The more you look, the more you see.

My work evolves from feelings triggered by sights in my immediate environment. Animal images are always present because, for me, animals are both teachers and healers. In them I sense an awareness and knowledge which guides me to a primitive core which is more than a personal experience. I express these elemental feelings that have no words.

Roxana Bartlett
Boulder, Colorado

The Wind Does Not Require the Grass to Answer
69.5″ x 69.5″

Cotton sateen, cotton velvet, canvas, acrylics, Procion™ dye

Dyed, pieced, appliquéd, painted, tied with perle cotton

Jill Pace
Glendale, Arizona

The Way Through
66″ x 66″

Cotton fabrics, beads, embroidery floss

Machine-pieced, hand-quilted, embroidered, beaded

I believe that we all have a "divine plan" ordained for each of our lives—a "dream" that is given to us. On the path to the discovery of our true vocation we often encounter obstacles, road blocks, and many challenges. With faith and hard work we can always find a way around obstacles. Our "finding a way" often makes us stronger, and enables us to project ourselves creatively back into the world.

Quilting is the language with which I express some of the changing concepts, ideas, and dreams in my life…a way of expanding myself into the world. Hand work on the surface of my quilts allows me to put some of my soul into each piece. Of all the things I have accomplished in my lifetime, it is when I am quilting that I feel I am truly living in the color of my dreams.

This pulchritudinous female is precariously perched in a typical starlet stance on the prow of Botticelli's shell from his wonderful *Birth of Venus* painting. This scene illustrates my impressions of Hollywood's plastic history. Will she fall from grace by displaying her remarkable talents on the film director's couch? The many dangers of her voyage are reflected in the rocky water. *Catch a Falling Star* signifies success by Hollywood standards. A lifetime love of movies and puns dictated the title.

Barbara W. Watler
Hollywood, Florida

Catch a Falling Star
50″ x 72″

Lamé, cotton, blends, velvet, metallic and rayon threads, ribbon floss

Hand-painted with Deka® silk dyes, embellished using colored pencils and thread; elements individually stitched, hand- and machine-appliquéd

Mildred (Millie) Sorrells
Macomb, Illinois

Monsho
77″ x 96″

Hoffman cotton fabrics, muslin, Hobbs® gray batting

Needle-turn-appliquéd, hand-quilted

Monshos are Japanese family crests. The monsho is a device which began simply to add identity and decorative signs of wealth and influence to clothing and carriages. These early designs were based on simple objects that brought beauty to life such as butterflies, flowers, and other plants.

My collection of 2- to 2.5-inch floral designs, from *Traditional Japanese Crest Designs* (Dover), were enlarged on a copy machine to 16 inches and then transferred to muslin blocks. I used the cutwork and the needle-turn method to appliqué the designs to the background fabric. For the border I took the spray from one of the blocks and added the Hanabishi, the diamond-shaped flower.

I liked the circular floral designs and I love to do needle-turn appliqué.

One of a series, *95-3: Blue* is a part of a search for a way to describe the essential mystery of textile. It is an attempt, through deliberate simplification, to reveal the spirit of each piece of cloth, to discover how each relates to each, and joins together to form a chorale of intense spirituality.

Jonathan Shannon
Belvedere, California

95-3: Blue
74″ x 74″

New and old commercial cotton fabrics

Machine-pieced, hand-quilted, tied

Robin Schwalb
Brooklyn, New York

Hear the Difference
36″ x 48″

Commercial and hand-dyed cottons and silk

Stenciled, photo silk-screened,
hand-dyed, machine-pieced, hand-appliquéd,
hand-quilted

Carefully constructed to look deconstructed, inspired by urban walls covered with layered, ripped, and weathered posters, this piece is full of references to sound, music, and sound reproduction. The Japanese ideogram means "ear" or "hearing." The quotation stenciled on the bottom layer refers to a young Siberian tribal woman who laughed and cried with excitement upon hearing her own voice recorded and played back to her. The repeating, silk-screened photo images show the same combination of fear and joy lighting up the face of Nanook of the North as he listens to a wind-up Victrola (in Flaherty's 1922 documentary). Nowadays we take machines so much for granted that we've lost the sense of wonder that they ought to inspire in us.

Hoop skirts were fashioned to restrict and confine motion and emotion. Yet in *Triplets* the hoops are expressive and mobile. Similarly letters, which are formal elements of language, are given new treatment, as seen above the hoops. Rigid structural elements are inverted into their opposite.

Rachel Brumer
Seattle, Washington

Triplets
55″ x 55″

Pima cotton, commercial cotton, pastel dye sticks, fabric paint, fabric sensitizer, cotton batting

Machine-pieced, hand-appliquéd, hand-quilted, contact-printed, stamped, top-stitched

Barbara Lydecker Crane
Lexington, Massachusetts

Tree and Leaf
47″ x 63″

Cotton fabrics, some hand-painted, polyester batting

Hand-appliquéd, hand-embroidered, hand-quilted

In this quilt I enjoyed creating light and shadow effects, hoping to suggest both form and symbolism.

The distant poplar tree casts a giant light in place of a shadow. This reflected shape is also a leaf, whose green veins continue into the aqua rivers of the surrounding landscape. The glow of the leaf shape in contrast with the gray threatening sky and the tree bending in the wind suggests that even in adversity, serendipity and grace are always possibilities.

In my work I try to express my wonderment for the natural world and its ultimate mystery of life.

Moons of Jupiter is a syncopated play of color, pattern, and progressions. During the design process I consider how each color impacts those around it and the work as a whole, how patterns move across the surface of the quilt, and the relative significance of shapes as they become unifying elements or isolated punctuation in the composition. I find watching the design emerge as I work on my pin wall to be the most engaging part of the quilting process.

Bonnie Bucknam Holmstrand
Anchorage, Alaska

Moons of Jupiter
Four pieces, each 36″ x 36″

Commercial cotton fabrics, hand-painted fabrics by Patty Hawkins, metallic sheer fabrics, nylon tulle, polyester batting

Machine-pieced, raw-edge appliquéd with metallic and decorative threads, machine-quilted

Ann Johnston

Lake Oswego, Oregon

Balancing Act III

55.5″ x 57.5″

Cotton broadcloth, hand-dyed cotton batting, cotton thread

Hand-dyed, machine-pieced, machine-quilted

I have a particular concept in mind that is sometimes specific, sometimes broad, with each quilt I make. I consider each quilt a step in preparation for the next, a learning process. For years part of this process has involved dyeing my own fabric, and frequently the fabric itself is a source of inspiration for the design and structure of a quilt.

While *Balancing Act III* had a specific content when I made it, I did not want to limit its meanings either for myself or for others by defining its content too precisely. I enjoy knowing that it may mean something very different to another viewer, and I regret that I do not get to hear more often what that meaning may be.

The May 1991 cover of *Scientific American* displayed a computer-generated head of a cat that appeared to be done in little squares. This method was perfect for Mistletoe; she is a tortoiseshell and white cat whose coloration appears mainly as little specks.

The perfect opportunity to make a quilt arose in 1994 when Mistletoe underwent a radioactive iodine treatment for hyperthyroidism. She had to stay in the hospital for one week. By the time our cured pet came home, her sun-kissed image was arranged on my felt backboard. Of course, she sits on a quilt because that's what cats like to do. And, yes, she was a Christmas present to me, twelve years ago.

Liselotte (Lisa) Tan
La Jolla, California

My Sweet Mistletoe
48″ x 48″

Cotton fabrics

Machine-pieced, hand-appliquéd, hand-quilted

Marylou Pepe
Boalsburg, Pennsylvania

Colors of High Resolve
102″ x 60″

Commercial and hand-dyed fabrics, cotton crochet thread, polyester ribbon, polyester batting, cotton and decorative rayon quilting thread, Procion MX™ reactive dyes

Machine-pieced, hand-appliquéd, hand-couched, photo-screen-printed

I was prompted to design this quilt for the 75th anniversary of women's suffrage. The flag-within-a-flag design was chosen as a symbol of a group united by a common cause, struggling within a country which had fought for its own liberty. The pieced and embroidered stars represent the number of states at the time of ratification of the 19th amendment and the present. The border of bars and Xs in graduated values symbolizes the imprisonment of women denied the vote.

The script is President Wilson's April 2, 1917, War Message which was also used by the suffragists when they picketed the White House. The silk-screened images honor several important suffragists: Susan B. Anthony, Elizabeth Cady Stanton, Lucretia Mott, Lucy Stone, Carrie Chapman Catt, and Alice Paul.

Twilight Serenade/Music in the Tombs is part of a series inspired by my fifteen years working as an archaeological technical artist in Greece, Egypt, and Jordan. Illustrating pottery shards requires tedious repetitive activity similar to the process I have experienced in my thirty years of quilting. In this piece three large amphoras float in an architectural environment. It is not a place I have worked, but an allegorical representation of antiquity.

I view archaeology's quest for historical and cultural identity as a metaphor for the individual's search for identity. My interest in making art lies in finding the critical point where reality is abstracted and events of my existence meet universal experience. In this quilt I have created a contemplative object directing the viewer to consider where we come from as a civilization and as individuals.

Julia E. Pfaff
Richmond, Virginia

Twilight Serenade/Music in the Tombs
91″ x 47″

Zinc plate etchings, hand-dyed and painted cotton fabrics, Procion™ fiber reactive dyes, cotton batting; all fabrics and images created by the artist

Hand-appliquéd, machine-sewn, foundation quilted

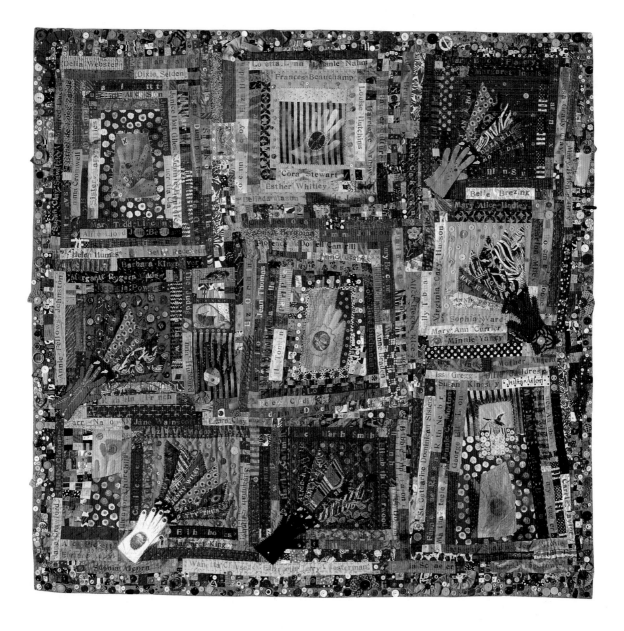

Jane Burch Cochran
Rabbit Hash, Kentucky

Coming Home: Kentucky Women Quilt
81″ x 78″

Cotton fabrics, gloves, old embroideries, beads, buttons, paint

Machine-pieced, hand-embellished, hand-quilted using embroidery thread; names stamped with acrylic paint and rubber stamps

Name quilts are a tradition in quiltmaking. This quilt contains over 200 names of Kentucky women, from the tribe names of early Native American cultures to names of today. A booklet listing the names and accomplishments fits in a pocket on the back of the quilt.

I decided to make this quilt as a change of pace and worked on it between other deadline quilts. Michelle Lustenberg and I stamped the names using a rubber stamp alphabet and acrylic paint on different strips of fabric. I constructed the quilt based on color and composition, and wanted the names to blend into the overall design. I used some old crazy quilt embroideries I found at a flea market and added the gloves to represent the different races and nationalities. The blue glove represents the blue people from Troublesome Creek, whose color was the result of a recessive gene.

Sunset Reflection is part of a series of sky reflections on water. The iridescent, lustrous quality of the silk relates to water's surface reflection of light. The image is quite abstract, as is an actual reflection on rippling water. The horizontal quilting mimics the rippling surface of water, and the cut vertical reverse appliqué strips resemble the reflected light and colors of the sky at sunset.

The technique of bias-cutting and pressing the entire top layer as well as many of the inner appliqués helps create the ripple/wave effect. A subtle sense of perspective is achieved by making wider rows at the bottom (foreground) and narrower rows at the top (background). Piecing was done by Shawn Behrends and Susan Hedin of the Harding Design Studio.

Tim Harding
Stillwater, Minnesota

Sunset Reflection
53″ x 59″

Duppioni silk surface and cotton backing

Multi-layered reverse appliqué

Leslie Gabriëlse
Rotterdam, The Netherlands

Arras/France
81″ x 79″

Cotton fabrics and acrylic paints

Appliquéd, stenciled, painted

I choose textiles for my medium because they allow for the playful surprises possible while working with the indigenous properties of the material—flexibility, color, and pattern.

From a distance the acrylic paint on this piece enhances the illusionary effect of a painting. The painterly effect is enhanced by the fabrics not being cut according to their representational shapes.

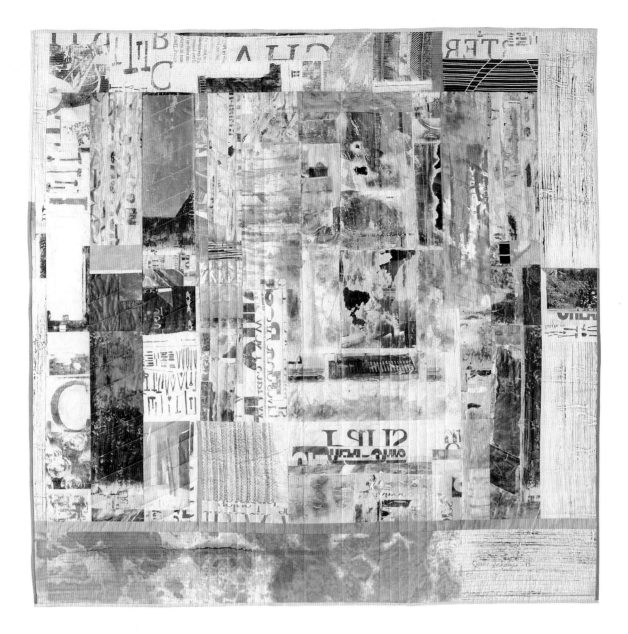

Part of an ongoing series, *Escape* is based on my travel in Italy. I am enamored with surfaces and how they disintegrate over time. I like the idea of layering and scratching away to reveal what is beneath the surface, much like the effect seen on old frescoes, illuminated manuscripts, and urban walls. These erasures and fragments are combined to say something about my experiences and ways of seeing.

Joan Schulze
Sunnyvale, California

Escape
60″ x 59″

Silk and cotton fabrics, paper

Photo-transfer printed, painted, pieced, appliquéd

Midge Hoffmann
Coburg, Oregon

Fall Into Winter
29″ x 36″

Duppionni silk

Hand-painted and stenciled, fused, machine-
stitched and machine-quilted

My recent studio work focuses on recurring graphic images and patterns in nature. I randomly paint, stamp, and stencil silk fabrics with spheres, spirals, snowflakes, crescents, and leaf and floral patterns. These are fractured by cutting up the fabrics and restructuring the forms into a new pattern, fusing and stitching the fabric to a backing. The spontaneously-painted fabric directs the new arrangement. Sometimes life seems fractured; sometimes, if we look closely, we see that life is actually made of a few basic swirling themes intrinsically woven together seeking balance and order in pattern and structure.

Fall Into Winter celebrates the change in seasons: the dark, cold sparkle of winter that descends onto the forest, gradually transforming the season before it.

Thread Bare II is the second quilt in a series depicting scenes of rural life in central Florida.

What my work is really about, though, is abstracting images, painting and printing on cloth, and reconstructing the cut pieces of fabric. This element of destruction and construction pops up a lot in my quilts.

Fran Skiles
Plantation, Florida

Thread Bare II
55″ x 53″

Cotton duck, rug canvas, fabric paint, waxed thread, buttons, toile, yarn, cassava resist

Photo silk-screened, photo-transferred, machine-embroidered, machine-appliquéd, machine-quilted

Becky Sundquist
Pinole, California

Arctic Light
30.5″ x 37.5″

Silk and cotton fabrics, birch bark, rayon and metallic threads, beads

Designed on the computer and printed directly on fabrics, machine-pieced, machine-appliquéd, free-motion machine-embroidered, machine-quilted

In the tradition of bringing life experiences to art, a moment captured in time and place held in memory is expressed here in fabric and texture. *Arctic Light* is the first in a World Journey series. The series is inspired by my trip around the world, a 300-day journey through 23 countries. It represents places explored and cultures experienced.

The design is based on a photograph that I took at the Arctic Circle in Finland. The quality of light at that latitude has a very special aura. I wanted to express the color and light of the Arctic with the periwinkle and rose of the midnight sun, the soft greens of the tundra grass, and the dancing light of the aurora borealis.

My special thanks go to Katie Pasquini Masopust for her inspiration and encouragement.

Small pieces of truth and beauty can be uncovered if one simply holds still and pays attention. I like to pretend that I had deduced this through spiritual self-exploration and the resulting wisdom. However, the truth is that the title of this work was the result of a traffic jam on a rainy night. I was anxious and irritable and in no mood for an epiphany. The only thing to be done was to stare resentfully at the reflections of buildings on the glossy asphalt.

Unexpected beauty is the most satisfying.

Sally A. Sellers
Vancouver, Washington

When You Are Very Still
79″ x 48″

Acrylic-stained canvas, metallic and synthetic fibers

Machine-appliquéd

Ritsuko Oikawa
Tokyo, Japan

Wintry Blast
40″ x 40″

Cotton, Japanese menswear kimono fabric

Cut and pieced, using a technique learned from
the artist's teacher Shizuko Kuroha

I love Japanese cotton indigos and I have many of
these old fabrics. Recently I started using stripes in my
work. *Wintry Blast* is the third piece in which these
stripes were used. When the cutting line is curved, the
stripes also look curved. This effect is emphasized
further by the quilting lines.

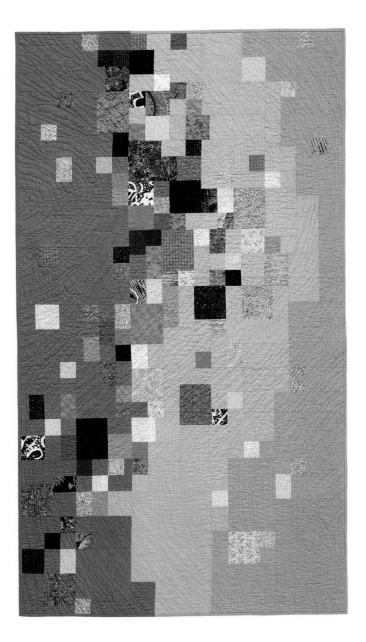

Dewey Beach is a shallow bay at the northern edge of Puget Sound where the tide moves great distances twice a day. Having recently moved from an over-crowded metropolitan city, daily life along this rural seashore fired my imagination. I was inspired to capture in my quilts impressions of the scene around me: goldfinches at my feeder; the watery world of Dungeness crabs; and beach rocks deposited by the waves in broad curves where the wet sand met the dry.

With *Beach Rocks* I am attempting to show that, although the beach can seem totally gray on an overcast day, it is transformed into a colorful scene by concentrating on the beauty and texture of the individual rocks. The quilting design imitates the pattern of ripples that wind creates on the surface of shallow water.

Heather W. Tewell
Anacortes, Washington

Vignettes of Dewey Beach: Beach Rocks
40″ x 69″

Cotton fabrics, cotton thread, cotton/polyester batting

Pieced, half-seam-pieced, hand-quilted

Helen Giddens
Rainbow, Texas

Al
108″ x 108″

Cotton fabrics, cotton/polyester batting,
sheet backing

Machine-pieced and machine-quilted

While doing a series on animals close to me, I included my beloved cat Al. He was my studio cat since I found him in a dog pound seven years ago. He was taken from me recently (I don't know who took him.) He was my buddy and I miss him a great deal. The quilt is made totally from scraps, as are all of my quilts. I like to make something out of throwaways, leftovers, out of nothing. Al was like that—he went from being a throwaway kitty to the best twenty-pound friend I ever had.

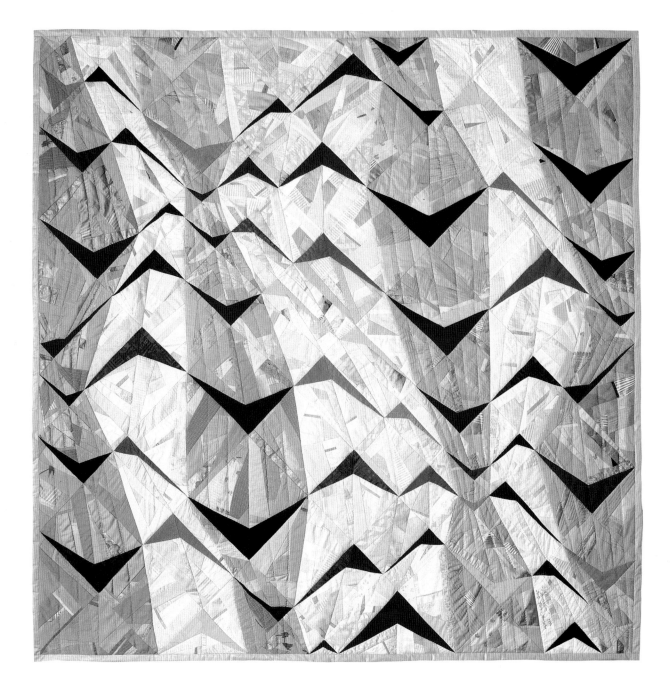

I get optical movement effects by narrowing the blocks. A formation of flying geese, small and large, narrow and wide, is constructed over the whole quilt.

Dorle Stern-Straeter
Muenchen, Germany

Formation
68″ x 68″

Cotton and silk fabrics

Crazy quilt technique

Libby Lehman
Houston, Texas

Haywire
48″ x 36″

Hand-dyed fabrics, rayon and metallic threads,
Fairfield Soft-Touch® batting

Machine-pieced, free-motion quilted, thread-
painted, bobbin-drawn, bobbin-couched

Haywire is part of a series called Threadplay in which
decorative threads are the major design element rather
than just embellishment.

The year 1995 marked the 50th year since the first explosion of the atom bomb. J. Robert Oppenheimer, Director of the Manhattan Project at Los Alamos, has become a symbol of the creation of the atom bomb. This was a pivotal event, momentous and devastating to some and exhilarating to others, even for the 20th century. For me, his portrait symbolizes the conscience of the country that used the bomb on a populated area. This image of him is very compelling: he seems to be looking in an open, questioning way and also in a self-searching way. He is receptive to what happened and responsible for the role he had in it. He opposed the development of the later hydrogen bomb and worked to stop the resulting arms race. In his last year he became somewhat of a tragic figure—at once famous and infamous.

Linda MacDonald
Willits, California

Portrait of J. Robert Oppenheimer
43.5″ x 49″

Cotton fabric and cotton batting

Dyed, airbrushed, painted, stitched

Jane Dunnewold
San Antonio, Texas

Seeking Order
87″ x 48″

Cotton fabrics, paints

Hand-painted, silk-screened, machine-appliquéd,
machine-quilted

I have been trying to make quilted surfaces which are more "painterly." To this end, *Seeking Order* is part of a series where I seek to introduce a sense of order into an otherwise spontaneous and rather chaotic background.

I am also recognizing the undeniable connection between "art" and "life," since I am constantly struggling to bring order to a rather chaotic existence.

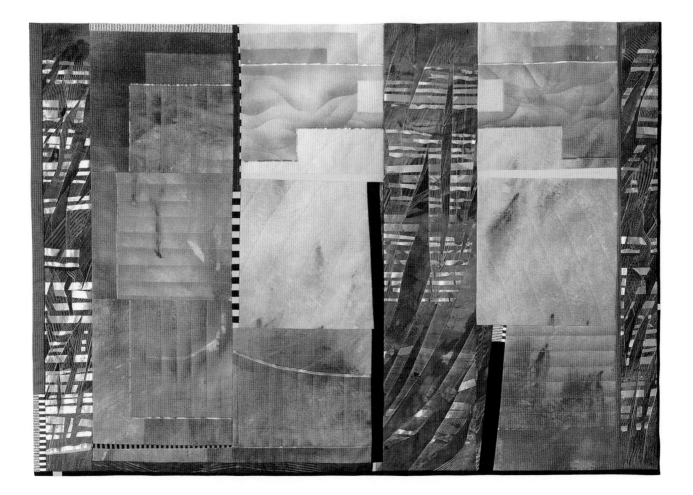

Transformation is the result of being "stuck" with a 6′ x 9′ already-quilted work. This large finished piece hung in my studio, haunting me with its deadness until one day I had the courage to cut it up! As if by magic, five new quilts evolved, Transformation being one of them. My willingness to let go of "safe" and risk all was rewarded with a whole new approach to my work.

Elizabeth A. Busch
Glenburn, Maine

Transformation
62″ x 43″

Canvas, acrylic paint, textile inks, metal leaf on acetate, commercial fabric, ribbon

Hand-painted, air-brushed, machine-pieced, hand- and machine-quilted

Terrie Hancock Mangat
Cincinnati, Ohio

Barbara Johnson, Over the Rhine
35" x 72"

Cotton fabric, leather, buttons, ostrich eggshell beads, cowrie shell luck charms, embroidery thread, acrylic paint

Embroidered, reverse-appliquéd, pieced and painted

When I moved into my studio in Over the Rhine three years ago, I noticed the friction between the local residents and the artists. To help people get to know each other, Patsy Bonafair and I organized a Summer Art Camp. We invited the artists to do art projects with the local children. This was the beginning of my education about the culture, the difficulties, and the beauty of the people living in this area.

The children are so hopeful and so resilient, in spite of lives edged with poverty, drugs, and violence. They soak up every ounce of attention, time, and opportunity offered them. My sister Becky Hancock and I have opened a fabric and bead store in the old historical area. Children stop by daily to do art projects, read books, and write journals.

This quilt is a part of the work I did with the children on an Individual Artists Grant from the city of Cincinnati. These children are so lovely. I wish for them better education and peaceful, productive lives.

The Gospel According to the Choir was created out of my love for the human face.

It seems to me that of all the ways people get together to form groups, singing together is the most joyous. I tried to convey that joy in this piece, from the serene look on the leader's face, to the eyes of the singers closed in ecstasy, to the clapping hands on the top of the quilt.

The colored strips of fabric represent the stained glass windows in the church where one might find this group. The pose of the central figure resembles that of Christ on the cross, a subject that I am sure this choir would sing about often. It is also represented in the architecture of the great cathedrals.

This is a piece about joy.

Rebekka Seigel
Owenton, Kentucky

The Gospel According to the Choir
68″ x 98″

Cotton and cotton-blend fabrics, embroidery floss

Machine-pieced, hand-appliquéd, embroidered, hand-quilted

Kiyoko Goto
Sendai Miyagi, Japan

Log Cabin II
78″ x 90″

Cotton and silk fabrics

Hand-pieced, machine-pieced, hand-quilted

Log Cabin II is the second in a series of log cabin quilts I have made. I love needlework and quiltmaking because it enables me to express myself. I love using old Japanese fabrics in my work.

When I made this piece I was thinking about what some women will do to make life run smoothly for their mates. Some iron; some don't. I prefer to let the dryer do the work for me.

Wendy Huhn
Dexter, Oregon

Joy of Ironing
47″ x 47″

Cotton fabrics, suede cotton fabric, Thermolam® batting, rick-rack, beads, Shisha mirrors, paint

Machine-pieced and quilted, photocopied images, stenciled, gel-transferred, mono-print stamped, rubber-stamped, sponge-painted, hand-appliquéd

Patricia Autenrieth
Hyattsville, Maryland

Starry Night
82″ x 59″

Cottons and blends, Pellon® fleece, batting

Silk-screened, mono-printed, enamel-sprayed,
painted, zigzag quilted

I keep telling myself that my use of the figure is a temporary aberration. I am at heart a landscape artist. Let's say, then, that my figures exist in psychological landscapes, surrounded by the flora and fauna peculiar to their environments.

My preferred technologies are drawing and printmaking. In *Starry Night* I simultaneously quilt and draw with the sewing machine. I also have silk-screened twenty-seven separate monoprints from trash I've picked up off the street in my own approach to recycling.

Our lives move through a course of tangled twists and turns, often detouring down unfamiliar paths, undesired routes, or to uncomfortable locations. One is forced to respond, ready or not, to a loss, a love, an unexpected light.

Our multi-faceted personalities shift in color and hue, traveling through time, sometimes changed forever. This piece reflects one of those unsettling periods, and the courage summoned to face it.

Patricia Kennedy-Zafred
Pittsburgh, Pennsylvania

Innocenza Presa
16.5″ x 21.5″

Acetate, hand-dyed fabrics by
Jan Myers-Newbury, vinyl, polyester batting, rayon and metallic threads

Machine-pieced and quilted

Susan Shie and James Acord
Wooster, Ohio

Fiesta Ware Quilt
54″ x 87″

Fabric paint, leather, clay beads, gemstones, floral marbles, pennies, and various other embellishments

Hand-painted, air-brushed, appliquéd, beaded, hand- and machine-embroidered, diary-written, leather-tooled, embellished with hand-sculpted clay

Courtesy of Mobilia Gallery,
Cambridge, Massachusetts

Fiesta Ware Quilt is a 1995 spring and summer diary of our lives. It is mixed with visual images and written stories of our love for Fiesta Ware, that joyous, many-colored dinnerware which is so fun to set the table with. Adventures chronicled here include: growing pumpkins and garden angst; Mom losing her glasses over and over at the nursing home; Dad's cataract surgery; cleaning the water well at Mom and Dad's house; and throwing a prosperity party for Gretchen and Mike—complete with cactus goblets for margaritas.

Visual delights include two versions of the Fiesta Ware Dancing Señoritas, cornbread heads, raspberry tea, and that sweet little embroidered poem about the mermaid and the parrot. Jimmy's leather teacups and teapots and Susan's ceramic art buttons (patio owls, turtles, etc.) dance all around the borders. Enjoy!

Over six hundred commercially printed fabrics were used in *Terrazzi*. The fabrics with clearly defined patterns were the most unpredictable in their visual effect. This contributed to a random yet controlled building process. After brighter fabrics were added, the splashes of color and pattern took on a life of their own. They began to describe geographic shapes: valleys, bodies of water, and cascading terraces.

Angela Dawson Woolman
Albany, California

Terrazzi
44″ x 53″

Cottons, linen, cotton batting, rayon thread

Machine-pieced, machine-quilted

Paula Nadelstern
Bronx, New York

KALEIDOSCOPIC XV:
Eccentric Circles
59″ x 75.5″

Cotton and silk fabrics, painted cotton by
Skydyes®

Machined-pieced, hand-quilted

There are two kinds of surprises: the meticulously planned kind and the happy coincidence. Making kaleidoscope quilts allows me to synthesize elements of both, to merge control and spontaneity to spark something unexpected. Light, color, form, and motion are juggled in every kaleidoscopic image, capturing a moment of infinity and offering a glimpse of order conquering chaos.

The impression of circles and curves is an illusion created by piecing straight lines. There is an air of abracadabra when the last seam is stitched because the whole is truly greater than the sum of its parts. And in the end, I get to be the one who makes the magic and the one who is surprised.

I'm impelled by the energy of color, and quiltmaking has both fueled and satisfied this intense interest. *The Dance* was made for a friend who is a dancer, choreographer, and yoga instructor. She requested the deep reds and the saturated hues. I had in mind her grace, humor, and style of energy as I worked.

There is a life force in all of this radiant color; it is the energy that exists in the great dance.

Rebecca Rohrkaste
Berkeley, California

The Dance
72″ x 72″

Commercial and hand-dyed cotton fabrics, cotton batting

Machine-pieced, machine-quilted

Diana Whitmer-Francko
Oxford, Ohio

Many Moons Over Serpent Mound
43″ x 58.25″

Cotton fabrics, dyes, paints, copper, Petoskey stones, beads, and buttons

Over-dyed, printed, reverse appliquéd, embellished with hand-fabricated copper figures and hand-made stone buttons, machine-pieced, hand-quilted

Prehistoric artifacts, mounds, and earthworks are the basis for a series of quilts I've been creating about ancient cultures. The mound builder culture of southern Ohio made numerous earthworks and artifacts to celebrate the natural and spirit worlds. One of these, a gigantic earthwork called Serpent Mound, is the inspiration for this quilt. Through this work I have tried to express my awe and admiration for the people who toiled to create it so "many moons" ago.

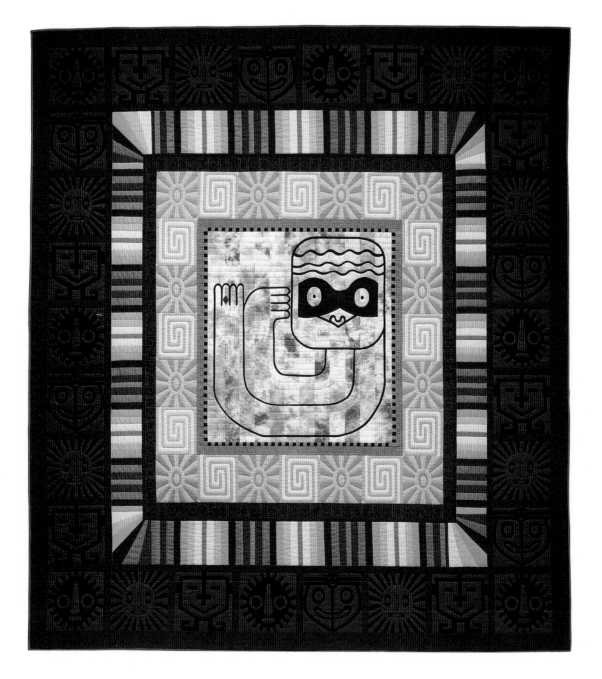

The figures in this quilt, including the central medallion, are screen-printed by hand. I frequently use screen printing in designing my quilts because the color and design possibilities are essentially unlimited. The central figure was inspired by an illustration in a book on Peruvian primitive art. Further research on the subject yielded other figures that appear in the quilt as well as a color scheme based on the weavings.

Hallie H. O'Kelley
Tuscaloosa, Alabama

Peruvian Primitive
75″ x 84″

Printed cotton fabrics, polyester batting

Machine-pieced, hand-quilted, using hand-dyed and screen-printed fabric

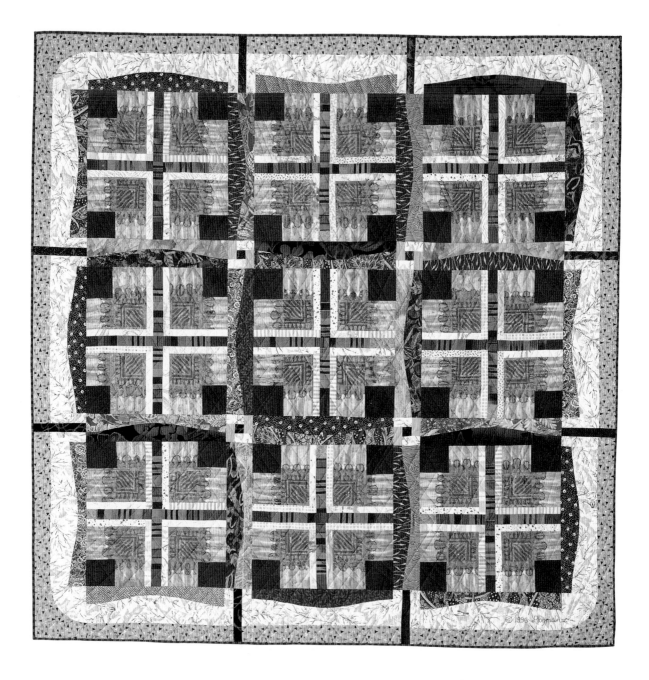

80

Elaine Plogman
Cincinnati, Ohio

African Crosses
63″ x 63″

Cotton, cotton-blend and
rayon fabrics, printing block designed and carved
by the artist's husband Robert Plogman

Block-printed, air-brushed, machine-pieced,
machine-quilted

African Crosses came from a desire to use a wonderful tie-dyed African fabric given to me by a friend and a printing block designed and carved by my husband. The printing block pattern dictated the formation of crosses. Working out the rest of the simple composition and selecting fabrics was a joy. It was one of those quilts that simply "flow."

In 1993 my husband and I moved to a classic 1950s California-modern home. It is a house I'd driven by often, hoping that "someday" we'd own it. Two long walls of full-height glass face a large paved and landscaped courtyard, blurring the distinction between indoors and out. We can watch the birds and squirrels (and, occasionally at night, raccoons!) from our living room. The courtyard is enclosed on the other two sides by a curved, perforated-brick screen wall that allows us to see out to the road, while blocking the view into our courtyard to those passing by.

Within/Without 3 is part of a series of quilts about walls and other barriers, visible and invisible, solid and permeable.

Liz Axford
Houston, Texas

Within/Without 3
80″ x 53″

Cotton fabrics and cotton batting

Hand-dyed, machine-pieced, machine-quilted

Barbara Sweeney
Montreal, Quebec, Canada

Violence Against Women
36″ x 45″

Cotton fabrics

Silk-screened, discharged white faces and images, painted, burned

My love for life and my curiosity and concern about people, as well as my love affair with cloth, is the essence of my art work. Cloth gives me the freedom to work in three dimensions and to use the surface for painting. Cloth provides endless possibilities for me to express my creativity.

Quilts are an excellent medium for me to communicate my feelings about the injustices (oppression, violence, and other abuse) that are done to women and children.

Life, people, and cloth will continue indefinitely, and so will my curiosity, concern, and love for all three.

Markers was conceived in a graveyard at the Taos Pueblo in New Mexico. The spiritual presence was overwhelming, and I was awestruck by a sense of the ancient souls resting there. The intensity of the experience surprised and energized me. It remained with me during the long drive home to Ohio. *Markers* is the second in a series about Taos and New Mexico.

Anne Triguba
Lancaster, Ohio

Markers
32″ x 39″

Cotton fabrics

Machine-pieced, hand-appliquéd, hand-quilted by Mary Shaffer under direction by the artist

M. Joan Lintault
Carbondale, Illinois

The Other Messengers
84″ x 108″

Cotton muslin, machine lace

Hand-dyed, hand-painted, screen-printed,
machine-quilted

I have begun a series of quilts called The Evidence of Paradise. I think there are indications of paradise all around us; we just need to know where to look and what to look for.

I would like to construct the character of nature and paradise from its smaller parts. I want to reveal the Japanese idea of mono-no-aware, the "pathos of things" and the poignancy inherent in a garden. It is the idea that a garden is the achievement of perfection before the beginning of decline and decay.

This quilt is a symbolic garden and, like all gardens, even in paradise, there are things to be discovered; but you must beware.

Madre de Deus is one in a series based on a trip I made to Portugal. It was inspired by a small church that is heavily encrusted with tile and gilded woodwork. I was overwhelmed with the powerful sense of belief I felt in this space, and that is what *Madre de Deus* is about.

Toot Reid
Tacoma, Washington

Madre de Deus
56.5″ x 71″

Cotton, rayon, silk fabrics, cotton batting

Machine-pieced, hand-appliquéd, hand-quilted

Deborah Melton Anderson
Columbus, Ohio

Shower
32″ x 49″

Cotton twill fabric, cotton thread, colored pencils

Photo transfers printed by a color laser copier, heat pressed onto the fabric

A shower…The sensation of a shower…A patterned tile wall…

Sources of inspiration for this piece are technique and pattern studies. The technique is tucked fabric, which acts as a resist when transfers are pressed onto it. The pattern is a modified repeat pattern found in 2000-year old Peruvian textiles. These ancient textiles have survived because they were buried with the dead in the coastal desert of Peru where a shower might not fall for several years.

"Photographic prints," made mostly of painted metal surfaces which have sustained scratches and splashes and now are rusting and peeling, were also used.

A red, white, and blue Fourth of July shower? No. A shower in Cuzco? Not likely. A shower stall in a dumpster? Hardly. Just a shower.

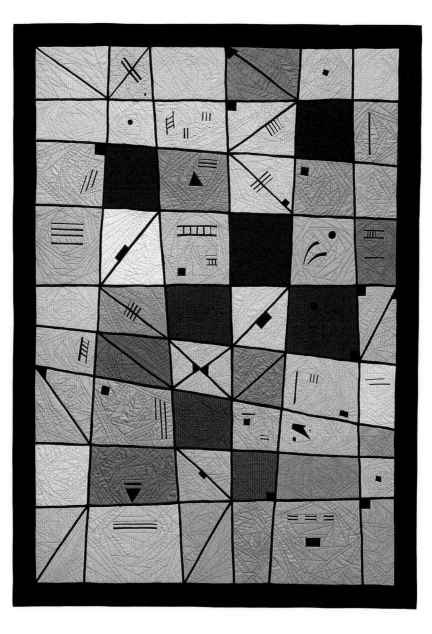

I approach crazy quilting as a technique that will add texture and movement to my designs. My quilts do not contain the embellishment usually associated with crazy quilting, since my interest is in the interaction between graphics of a design and texture of the created fabric.

My fascination with contemporary crazy quilting has lasted for more than twenty years, so I think of my crazy quilts as an ongoing series. I regard the technique as one of many in my repertoire and turn to it when it will help me solve a design problem. Or, sometimes, just because I want to work with it again!

Soho Sunday was inspired by a small Kandinsky watercolor that I saw in the Soho branch of the Guggenheim Museum one rainy Sunday when I was in New York.

Dixie Haywood
Pensacola, Florida

Soho Sunday
50″ x 67″

Cotton fabrics and batting

Contemporary crazy quilting, machine-pieced, machine-quilted, hand-appliquéd

The Artists

The Quilts

We received significant contributions from these corporate sponsors in producing this exhibition. We are very grateful for their financial assistance and their continuing interest in promoting the quilt as art.

Rosie's Calico Cupboard Quilt Shop, San Diego, California
Catering to quilters and crafters since 1983. Offering more than 6,000 bolts of first quality, 100%-cotton fabrics

P & B Textiles
Creator of 100%-cotton prints and solids that inspire and fulfill the needs of quiltmakers worldwide

Omnigrid®
Creating a Revolution in Rotary Cutting

Robert Kaufman Co., Inc.
Designer and manufacturer of fine Kona Cotton™ solids and unique 100%-cotton solids and prints

For information on other available books from C&T Publishing write to:
C&T Publishing
P.O. Box 1456
Lafayette, CA 94549
(1-800-284-1114)